Moving House

On moving day a huge removal van arrives very early. The men load all the furniture and lots of packing cases into the van.

Soon it is time to wave goodbye to the old house.

bookcase

drawers

kennel

carpet

packing case

lampshade

sofa

piano

lamp

bed

mattress

stool

sign

removal van

garden seat

postman

letters

window cleaner

removal man

ladder

shopping trolley

bucket

overalls

New Neighbours

When they arrive at their new home, all the neighbours are there to welcome them.

The man from next door has brought Mum a plant, and the boy from across the road has brought his new bike to show Peter.

Painting and decorating

One of the rooms in the house needs decorating. Mum suggests that Dad should paper the wall, but Dad isn't too sure!

Some of the twins' friends are helping too.

hooks

window frame

windowpane

paintbrush

paint pot

window sill

radiator

skirting board

pipe

scraper

scarf

mat

brush

dustpan

fringe

polish

candlestick

cloth

feather duster

leather

spray

vacuum cleaner

curtain rail

light bulb

door frame

pattern

wall

door

duster

apron

door handle

bucket

light switch

paste table

stepladder

wallpaper

folding table

socket

brush

floorboards

scissors

cupboard

"breaktime"

tea and cakes

In the kitchen

Today is the twins' birthday. "I am six today!" says Paul. "So am I!" giggles Polly.
Mum has made a splendid birthday cake for the party in the afternoon.

pepper

salt

cooker

pasta jar

oven

socket

plug

cable

kettle

cup

saucer

flame

candle

icing pump

kitchen towel

birthday cake

bun case

bread

breadboard

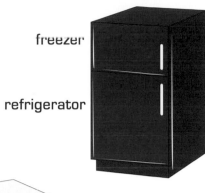
freezer

refrigerator

dishwasher

cake

high chair

mug

pan

plant

cookery book

taps

blind

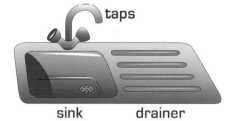
sink   drainer

curtains

knife

fork

plate

spoon

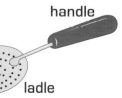
handle

ladle

jelly

yoghurt

jar

egg

carton

egg cup

The birthday party

While mum and dad get the tea, the children play "Hunt the Thimble".

The one who finds the thimble hides it the next time!

wall light

party hat

thimble

record player

present

bow

ribbon

gift tag

footstool

spotlight

radio

record

newspaper

balloons

photograph

video recorder

clock

armchair

magazine rack

cup

saucer

teapot

biscuits

rug

coffee table

fireguard

bookends

jug

cream cake

books

coffee pot

magazine

Baby's bedroom

That night Baby Patsy is the first to go to bed.

Patsy's jumping up and down in her cot. She doesn't look very tired, does she?

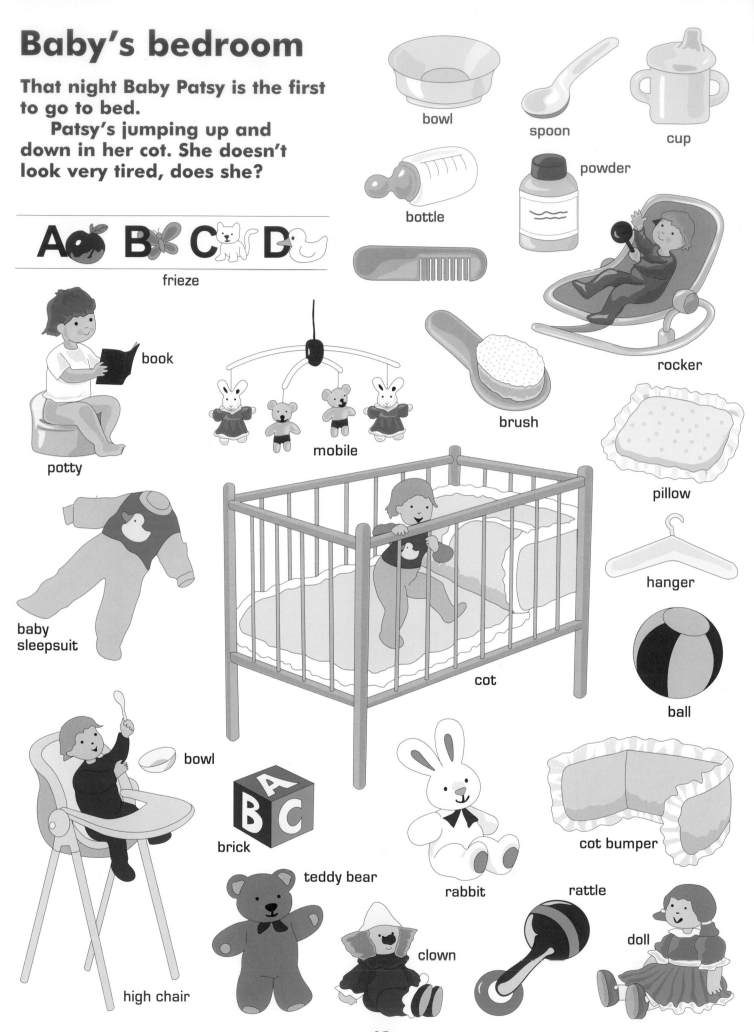

bowl

spoon

cup

powder

bottle

frieze

book

potty

baby sleepsuit

mobile

brush

rocker

pillow

hanger

ball

cot

bowl

brick

teddy bear

clown

rabbit

rattle

doll

cot bumper

high chair

The bathroom

Peter is having a bath before he goes to bed.

He's borrowed Patsy's toy duck to play with, but he wouldn't like anyone to know!

mirrror

scale

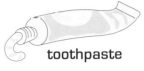
toothpaste

chain

shower

toilet roll

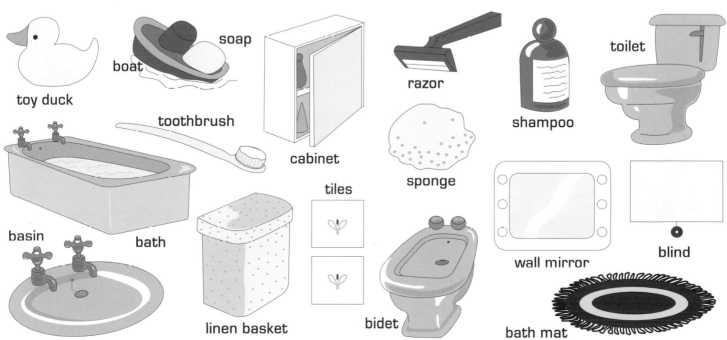

toy duck

boat

soap

toothbrush

cabinet

razor

shampoo

toilet

sponge

tiles

wall mirror

blind

basin

bath

linen basket

bidet

bath mat

- 13 -

Paul and Polly's bedroom

Polly is so tired after the party, she has gone to sleep straight away.......isn't her side of the room untidy!

Paul is still up, playing with his favourite present.

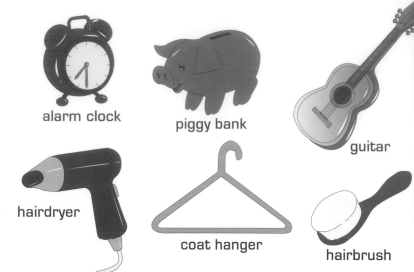

alarm clock

piggy bank

guitar

hairdryer

coat hanger

hairbrush

desk

poster

wardrobe

waste bin

duvet pillow

bed

chair

toy truck

radio

jeans

handbag

brick

lamp

The garage and workshop

Today Dad has asked the twins to help him in his worshop.
    Mum and Dad have a special present for Paul and Polly.
    Can you guess what it is?

rabbit hutch

plank

wire mesh

paintbrush

plant pots

paint pot

box

screws

saw

mallet

tape measure

rake

hoe

mower

fork

spade

garage door

watering can

shelves

pliers

nails

hook

ladder

shears

jigsaw

hacksaw

bench

shavings

screwdriver

sawdust

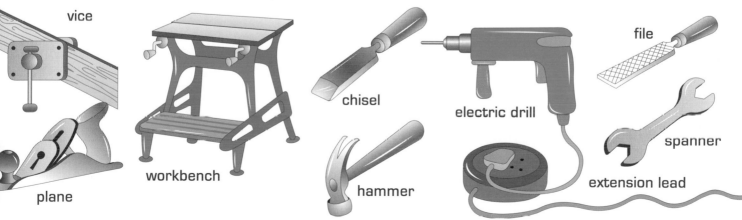

vice

file

workbench

chisel

electric drill

spanner

plane

hammer

extension lead

Our garden

Everyone is out in the garden - and there in the middle of the lawn is the surprise present ... a baby rabbit!

umbrella

shrubs

fence

plates

glass

table

greenhouse

lawn

onions

leaves

fork

trowel

rubber boots

wheelbarrow

cabbages

spade

wheel

hosepipe

soil

compost

bucket

spade

sandpit

post

creeper

gate

barbecue

patio door

bush

tub

chair

patio

cushion

bricks

reeds

bird

water lily

pond

bird table

stones

fish

cat

lettuce leaf

rabbit

water

hutch

lawnmower

flowers

cable

trellis

Here is a list of words you can learn about things around the house.

aerial
armchair
apple
attic
aquarium
alarm clock

bungalow
ball
bat
banana
bottle
butterfly
bedroom
bathroom
back garden
bin
baby
bushes
boy
bed
bucket
brush
bun case
bread
breadboard
blind
birthday cake
books
bookends
biscuits
balloons
brick
book
baby sleepsuit
bowl
boat
bookcase
bath
basin
bidet
bath mat
box
bench
bird

bird table
barbecue

Castle
coat hanger
cottage
can
clouds
chimney pot
chimney
cat
carpet
candlestick
cupboard
cable
cup
clock
cream
candle
carton
cookery book
curtain rail
cooker
cake
curtains
coffee pot
coffee table
cot bumper
creeper
cushion
chair
comb
chain
chisel
cabinet
cabbages
compost
cloth
clown

door
delivery van
drainer
drainpipe
duvet
duster
drain
drawers
desk
dishwasher

dustpan
door handle
door frame
doll

egg
egg cup
electric drill
extension lead

flats
farmhouse
fence
field
fringe
feather duster
folding table
floorboards
fork
flame
freezer
footstool
fireguard
frieze
file
flowers
fish

globe
garden seat
garage door
greenhouse
gutter
glass
guitar
gift tag
garden
gate

houseboat
hat
helmet
hall
handrail
hooks
handle
high chair
hair-brush

handbag
hanger
hoe
hammer
hacksaw
hosepipe

igloo
icing pump

jelly
jar
jug
jeans
jigsaw

ketchup
kitchen
kerb
kennel
kettle
kitchen towel
knife

log cabin
lawn
lampshade
lamp
letters
ladder
leather
light bulb
light switch
linen basket
ladle
lawnmower
lettuce
leaf
leaves

mug
mattress
mat
magazine rack
magazine
mirror
mallet

- 20 -

new house
nails
newspaper

Oven
old house
overalls
onions

porch
patio
potty
powder
present bow
poster
plane
plank
plant pots
pliers
post
pond
party hat
photograph
pot
pan
pram
pillow
pavement
packing case
post van
postman
piano
polish
pieces
piggy bank
paint
pipe
paste
pattern
pepper
pasta jar
plug
plate
paintbrush
plant
patio door

roof
railings

rocker
removal man
removal van
rug
radiator
ribbon
record
rabbit hutch
rake
record player
rubber boots
rocket
razor
refrigerator
radio
rattle
rabbit
reeds
road

Sofa
socket
streetlight
shrubs
steps
street name
stepladder
salt
spatula
spray can
suitcase
stairs
satellite dish
stroller
scarf
spray
skirting board
stool
scraper
scissors
saucer
sink
spoon
sign
sprout
scales
shower
semi-detached
shopping trolley
soap
sponge

spotlight
screws
spade
spanner
shelves
shears
shampoo
screwdriver
shavings
sawdust
soil
sandpit
stones
slabs
saw

terrace
trees
tiles
trellis
twins
toothbrush
toothpaste
taps
thimble
teapot
toy
tape measure
toilet roll
toy duck
toilet
teddy bear
travel
tub
truck
tea

Umbrella

Video
video recorder
vice
vacuum cleaner

Wigwam
washing
woman
window cleaner

window frame
windowpane
wall mirror
wire mesh
watering can
wheelbarrow
water lily
window sill
wallpaper
workbench
water
wheel
wardrobe
windows
wall
waste bin
wall light

yacht
yoghurt

tea

All sorts of jobs

butcher

chef

musician

mechanic

architect

businesswoman

businessman

photographer

weather girl

cameraman

vet

waiter

cowboy

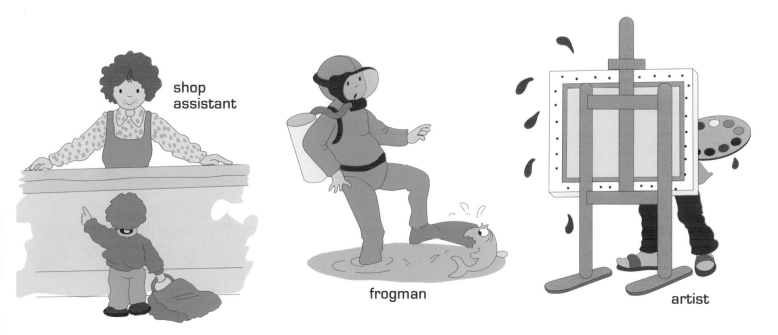

shop assistant

frogman

artist

carpenter

astronaut

librarian

fashion designer

model

messenger

fisherman

street cleaner

Let's look at people's jobs

Melanie, Sidney, Coral and Chloe, Jake, Fiona, Donald, Alice and Dickie were a group of friends in the same class at school, who set out to find out about other people's jobs.

Look at the clothes the people are wearing in the picture below. Can you guess what job each person does? Then try to find them in the book.

racket

spotlight

spanner

syringe

helmet

shoes

road drill

chicken

Match up the objects

Can you match them to the right person inside the picture?

'Remember to look out for me, Toby, in the pictures!'

- 25 -

A day on the farm

Melanie went to visit a farm. First she fed the chickens, then she fed the pigs.

Next she watched the farmer milk the cows, afterwards she had a ride on the tractor.

But best of all the farmer's daughter let Melanie ride her pony.

chicken

sheepdog

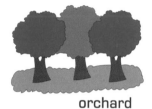
orchard

bales

combine harvester

chicks

cockerel

farmer

cow

milk tanker

horse

rider

goose

farmhouse

grain

trailer

tractor

farmer's wife

barns

gate

turkey

pig

hen house

stable

sheep

weathervane

duckling

duck

duck pond

A visit to the garage

Sidney's bike needed fixing. "I'll go to the garage and see my friend Mick the mechanic and he will tell me all about his job."

Mick was very busy trying to fix a car engine. He was using all sorts of tools and showed Sidney what each one was for.

He let Sydney look around the garage and last of all, he mended his bike.

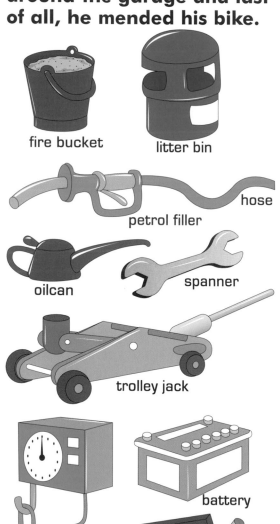

fire bucket

litter bin

hose

petrol filler

oilcan

spanner

trolley jack

air pump

battery

toolbox

screwdriver

mallet

pliers

trolley

helmet

oil filter

hook

pickup truck

car wash

car boot

rear light

petrol can

bumper

light

sticker

shop

hydraulic ramp

pit

bonnet

mechanic

motorbike

rider

trolley jack

overalls

engine

toolbox

watering can

bicycle

cyclist

extinguisher

petrol pump

air filter

no smoking sign

paper towel

wheel

A trip to the circus

As the circus was in town, Coral and Chloe thought they would find out about all the jobs in the big top.

They watched the trapeze artist flying high above the ring, and the bareback rider as she balanced on her beautiful pony.

Two funny clowns let Coral and Chloe help in their act - and even wear their baggy trousers.

lion tamer

whip

lion

pedestal

clown

conductor

baton

music

music stand

tights

trapeze

brass band

safety net

tent pole

bars

cage

gorilla suit

top hat

audience

clapping

jodhpurs

boots

tail-coat

big top

truck

cages

ringmaster

trapeze artist

balloons

string

ice cream

ring

pole

high wire rider

bareback rider

elephant

ball

ruff

dog

hoop

unicycle

horn

pony

water

bucket

popcorn

clown's car

clown

clubs

A day on the building site

Every day on the way to school Jake passed a busy building site. The big heavy machines that worked there made lots of noise and dust!

The foreman gave Jake a yellow hard hat and took him round the site.

He told Jake that he must never play on a building site or look round on his own - as it is very, very dangerous!

plan

helmet

spirit level

trowel

paint pot

brush

saw

float

cement

brick hammer

shovel

brick

'This is the best part of building!'

roof timbers

window

building

crane

cement mixer truck

cement

digger

- 32 -

counterweight

cab

tower crane

pulley

truck

steel girders

floor .... wood

bulldozer

insulation

walls

site office

joiner

painter

frame

cement mixer

sand

labourer

wheelbarrow

- 33 -

A visit to the dentist

Fiona didn't mind going to the dentist. When her examination was finished she asked the dentist how she looked after people's teeth.

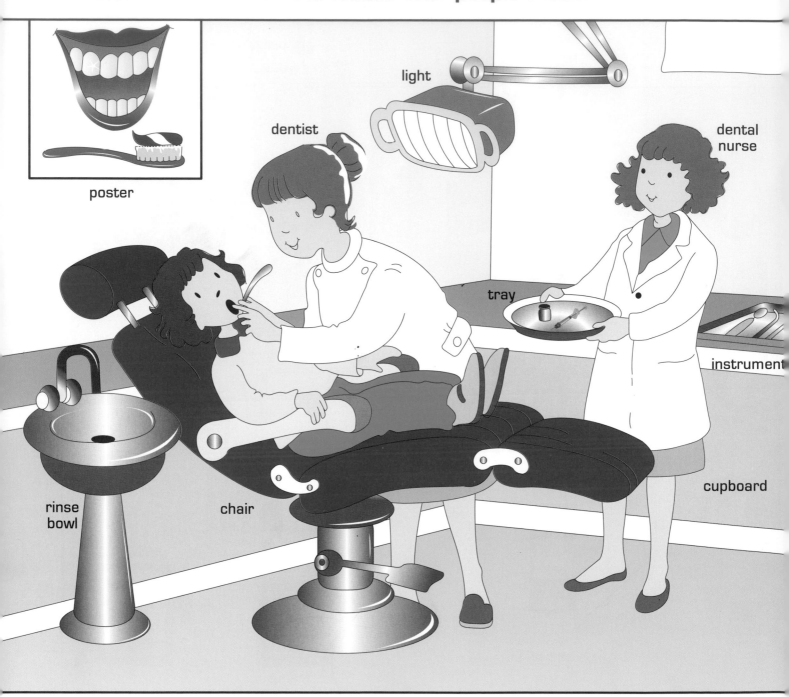

poster

light

dentist

dental nurse

tray

instrument

rinse bowl

chair

cupboard

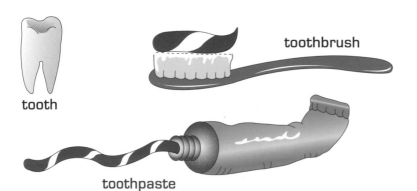

tooth

toothbrush

toothpaste

"Don't forget to brush your teeth every day to keep your smile nice and your teeth sparkly white!'

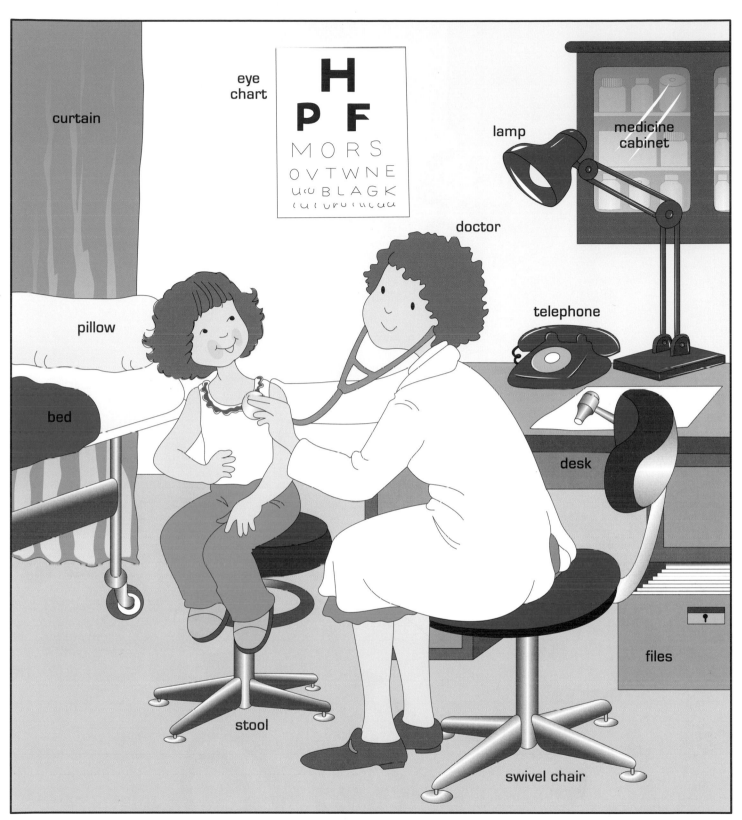

curtain

eye chart

H P F
M O R S
O V T W N E
u w B L A G K

lamp

medicine cabinet

doctor

telephone

pillow

bed

desk

files

stool

swivel chair

and the doctor

Fiona wanted to be a doctor like her mum, so she often went into her surgery to watch as she got on with her work.

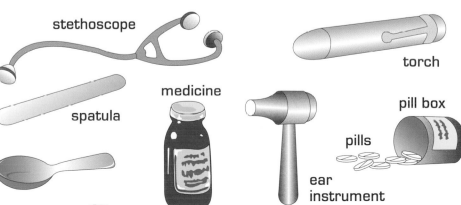

stethoscope

torch

spatula

medicine

pills

pill box

medicine spoon

ear instrument

screen

orange drink

chart

hat

nurse

tray

apron

wheelchair

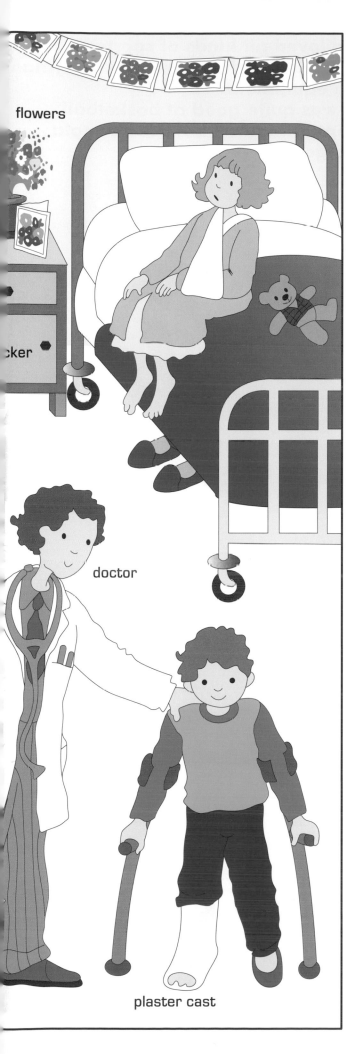

flowers

cker

doctor

plaster cast

Spending time in hospital

Sometimes Fiona went to hospital with her mum, so she was able to talk to the nurses and see how they took care of the patients.

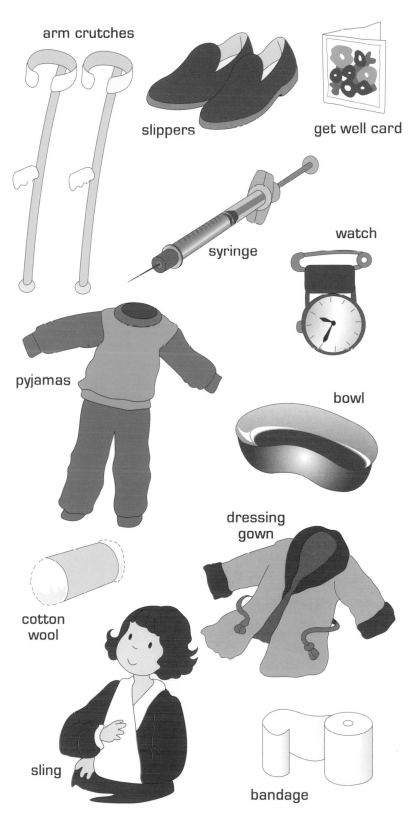

arm crutches

slippers

get well card

syringe

watch

pyjamas

bowl

dressing gown

cotton wool

sling

bandage

All sorts of sports

Donald loved all kinds of sports, so he spent his day at the sports centre trying out the equipment.

He was quite good at basketball, excellent at tennis - but poor Donald was no good at judo!

'I am going to be a rugby player.'

runner

ice hockey

pole vault

football

racing car

skiing

baseball bat

golf bag

judo suit

hockey stick

tennis racket

rugby ball

pole

weights

weightlifting

baseball

basketball

tennis

golf

volleyball

waterskiing

judo

trainer

ski goggles

football

basketball

water ski

helmet

'I think I will wait until I am a little bit bigger.'

spotlight

coloured light

wire

fairytale castle

spire

wings

crown

star

wand

painted backcloth

scenery

balcony

path

bird costume

footlights

stage

audience

seats

A night at the theatre

After the performance Alice went backstage.

"I'd love to be on the stage!" said Alice standing in the spotlight. "Shall I be a dancer or a singer, I really can't decide."

Then Alice heard the orchestra playing and listened to the audience clapping.

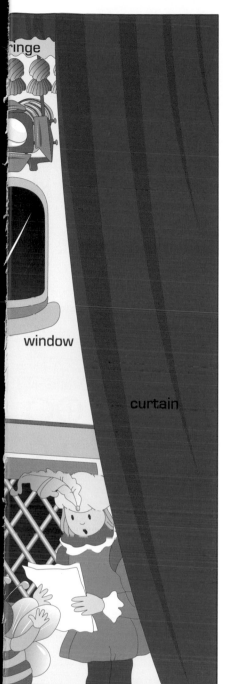

fringe

window

curtain

script

wig

ribbons

ballet shoes

powder puff

make-up brush

greasepaint

tutu

costume

mask

backstage

scene-shifter

actress

make-up girl

actor

script

People who help us

Dickie visited the fire station, and while he was there, the fire bell rang.

In no time at all, the fire crews jumped onto their fire engines and rushed to the fire, lights flashing and sirens wailing.

"I'd love to be a fireman," gasped Dickie, "it's so exciting!"

"False alarm!" the Fire Chief yelled. "It's only a barbecue!"

smoke

hedge

flashing lights

ladder

control valves

barbecue

fire chief

fire engine

hose

path

gate

flashing lights

police car

ambulance

blanket

step

stretcher trolley

policewoman

ambulance man

This boy has had a slight accident. The policewoman has sent for an ambulance to take him to hospital.

- 42 -

turntable ladder

tree

helicopter

pavement

grass

road

reel

If you have an accident at sea, the lifeboat will be launched and the brave crew will rescue you.

Sometimes they need to call in the helicopter to lift you to safety.

Here is Dickie taking part in an air sea rescue.

helmet

uniform

fireman

axe

water hydrant

Dickie's uncle is a security guard in a big store at night. Here he is with his fierce guard dog!

guard dog

torch

mast

radar

spotlight

crewman

rail

lifeboat

life raft

sea

foam

waves

Back at school

Melanie, Sidney, Carol and Chloe, Jake, Fiona, Donald, Alice and Dickie had a great time finding out about other people's jobs.

"Would any of you like to be a teacher?" asked Miss Tracey.

"Oh no!" they shouted all together.

alphabet cards

world map

palette

drawing pins

paintbrush

paint pot

pencils

plasticine model

cardboard model

water pot

felt-tip marker

chalk

board cleaner

teacher's desk

ruler

globe

aquarium

star

circle

square

shapes

work table

plasticine

waste bin

plant

plant pot

glue pot

apron

drawing

sums

pencil box

pencil sharpener

leaves

eraser

...... but some of them thought they would like to be dinner ladies, and give the children great, big dinners!

forks

knives

dinner lady

milkshake

Here is a list of words you can learn about all sorts of jobs.

architect
artist
astranaut
actress
air pump
air filter
audience
apran
actor
axe
ambulance
ambulance man
aquarium
alphabet cards
arm crutches

butcher
businessman
businesswoman
battery
bumper
barns
builder
bareback rider
ball
boots
bucket
balloon
bang
bonnet
band
bars
baton
big top
brush
bicycle
brick hammer
brick
bed
bales
bulldozer
building
bowl
bandage
baseball

baseball bat
basketball
balcony
bird costume
ballet shoes
backstage
barbecue
blanket
board cleaner

Chef
cameraman
cowboy
clown
carpenter
control valves
costume
chicken
cow
cockerel
combine harvester
chicks
car wash
car boot
clubs
cyclist
conductor
cage
clapping
clown's car
cement
counterweight
cement mixer
cement mixer truck
coloured light
crane
cab
chair
cupboard
curtain
chart
crown
cotton wool
crewman
cardboard
chalk
circle

duck pond
duck

duckling
dog
digger
dentist
dental nurse
doctor
desk
drawing
dressing gown
drawing pins
dinner lady

elephant
eye chart
engine
eraser
extinguisher

frogman
fashion designer
fisherman
farmhouse
farmer's wife
fire bucket
float
floor
frame
files
flowers
football
fringe
fairytale castle
footlights
fire chief
fire engine
flashing lights
foam
forks
felt-tip marker
fireman
farmer

grain
gate
goose
golf
golf bag
gorilla suit
glue pot

globe
glass
get well card
greasepaint
grass
guard dog

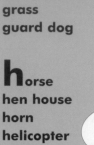

horse
hen house
horn
helicopter
hedge
hose
hook
hoop
hat
hydraulic ramp
high wire rider
hockey stick
helmet

ice cream
ice hockey
insulation

jodhpurs
joiner
judo
judo suit

knives

librarian
litter bin
light
lion
lion tamer
lamp
locker
ladder
lifeboat
leaves
labourer

musician
music